ANIMAL
NURSERY
RHYMES

This 1995 edition published by Derrydale Books
distributed by Random House Value Publishing, Inc.,
40 Engelhard Avenue, Avenel, New Jersey 07001.

Random House
New York ● Toronto ● London ● Sydney ● Auckland

A CIP catalog record for this book is available from the Library of Congress.

ISBN 0-517-12175-1

Printed and bound in China

ANIMAL NURSERY RHYMES

CHOSEN AND ILLUSTRATED BY
JOCELYN WILD

DERRYDALE BOOKS
NEW YORK · AVENEL

For my darling granddaughter Nancy
J.W.

It's raining, it's pouring,
The old man is snoring.
He went to bed
And bumped his head
And couldn't get up in the morning.

Hay is for horses,
Straw is for cows,
Milk is for little pigs,
And wash for old sows.

Intery, mintery, cutery, corn,
Apple seed and briar thorn;
Wire, briar, limber lock,
Five geese in a flock,
Sit and sing by a spring,
O-U-T, and in again.

Rain, rain, go away,
Come again another day,
Little Johnny wants to play.

One misty, moisty morning,
When cloudy was the weather,
I chanced to meet an old man
Clothed all in leather;
He began to compliment,
And I began to grin:
How do you do, and how do you do,
And how do you do again?

See-saw sacradown,
Which is the way to London town?
One foot up and the other foot down,
That's the way to London town.

Cut thistles in May;
They'll grow in a day.
Cut them in June;
They'll grow again soon.
Cut them in July;
Then they will die.

Row, row, row your boat, gently down the stream.
Merrily, merrily, merrily, merrily, life is but a dream.

Mother, may I go out to swim?
Yes, my darling daughter.
Hang your clothes on a hickory limb,
And don't go near the water.

Great A, little a,
Bouncing B.
The cat's in the cupboard,
And he can't see me.

Bell horses, bell horses,
What time of day?
One o'clock, two o'clock,
Three and away.

19

Old Abram Brown is dead and gone,
You'll never see him more;
He used to wear a long brown coat
That buttoned down before.

Bessy Bell and Mary Gray,
They were two bonny lasses;
They built their house upon the lea,
And covered it with rushes.

Bessy kept the garden gate,
And Mary kept the pantry;
Bessy always had to wait,
While Mary lived in plenty.

21

Davy Davy dumpling
Boil him in a pot.
Sugar him,
And butter him,
And eat him while he's hot.

22

One, two, three, four,
Mary at the cottage door;
Five, six, seven, eight,
Eating cherries off a plate.

Button to chin
When October comes in;
Cast not a clout
Till May be out.

25

If I'd as much money
As I could tell,
I never would cry,
Old clothes to sell!
Old clothes to sell!
Old clothes to sell!
I never would cry,
Old clothes to sell!

Manners in the dining room,
Manners in the hall,
If you don't behave yourself
You shan't have none at all.

Gregory Griggs, Gregory Griggs
Had twenty-seven different wigs.
He wore them up, he wore them down,
To please the people of the town.
He wore them east, he wore them west,
But he never could tell which he liked the best.

29

30

Who's that ringing at my door bell?
A little pussy cat that isn't very well.
Rub its little nose with a little mutton fat;
That's the best thing for a little pussy cat.

Doctor Foster
Went to Gloucester
In a shower of rain.

He stepped in a puddle
Right up to his middle
And never went there again.

Barney Bodkin broke his nose;
Without feet we can't have toes.
Crazy folks are always mad;
Want of money makes us sad.

Pease porridge hot,
Pease porridge cold,
Pease porridge in the pot,
Nine days old.

Some like it hot,
Some like it cold,
Some like it in the pot,
Nine days old.

37

Dingty diddlety,
My mommy's maid,
She stole oranges,
I am afraid.
Some in her pocket,
Some in her sleeve,
She stole oranges,
I do believe.

Blow, wind, blow,
And go, mill, go,
That the miller may grind his corn;
That the baker may take it,
And into bread make it,
And bring us a loaf in the morn.

40

Handy Pandy,
Jack a Dandy,
Loves plum cake
And sugar candy.
He stole some from the grocer's shop,
And out he came hop, hop, hop, hop.

41

At Brill on the hill
The wind blows shrill,
The cook no meat can dress;
At Stow-on-the-Wold
The wind blows cold,
I know no more than this.

42

Hoddley, poddley, puddle and fogs,
Cats are to marry the poodle dogs;
Cats in blue jackets and dogs in red hats,
What will become of the mice and the rats?

43

Ladybug, ladybug,
Fly away home,
Your house is on fire
And your children all gone.
All but one,
And that's little Ann;
And she has crept under
The frying pan.

Mr. Ibister, and Betsy his sister,
Resolved upon giving a treat;
So letters they write,
Their friends to invite,
To their house in Great Camomile Street.

46

47

The rose is red, the rose is white,
The rose is in my garden.
I would not part with my sweetheart,
For tuppence ha'penny farden.

48

Wash the dishes
Wipe the dishes
Ring the bell for tea.
Three good wishes
Three good kisses
I will give to thee.

The cat sat asleep by the side of the fire,
The mistress snored loud as a pig.
Jack took up his fiddle, by Jenny's desire,
And struck up a bit of a jig.

50

Ickle ockle, blue bockle,
Fishes in the sea,
If you want a pretty girl,
Please choose me.

Peter, Peter, pumpkin eater,
Had a wife and couldn't keep her;
He put her in a pumpkin shell,
And there he kept her very well.

Gee up, Neddy, to the fair,
What shall we buy when we get there?
A penny apple and a penny pear,
Gee up, Neddy, to the fair.

Dickery dickery dare,
The pig flew up in the air.
The man in brown
Soon brought him down,
Dickery dickery dare.

Charley Barley, butter and eggs,
Sold his wife for three duck eggs.
When the ducks began to lay,
Charley Barley flew away.

When Jacky's a good boy,
He shall have cakes and custard,
But when he does nothing but cry,
He shall have nothing but mustard.

Bat, bat, come under my hat,
And I'll give you a slice of bacon,
And when I bake,
I'll give you a cake,
If I am not mistaken.

Hokey, pokey whisky thum,
How d'you like potatoes done?
Boiled in whisky, boiled in rum,
Says the King of the Cannibal Islands.

Oh, rare Harry Parry,
When will you marry?
When apples and pears are ripe.
I'll come to your wedding,
Without any bidding,
And dance and sing all night.

Old Mother Hubbard
Went to the cupboard,
To fetch her poor dog a bone;
But when she got there
The cupboard was bare,
And so the poor dog had none.

62

63

Baa, baa, black sheep,
Have you any wool?
Yes, sir, yes, sir,
Three bags full;
One for the master,
One for the dame,
And one for the little boy
Who lives down the lane.

Round about, round about,
Maggotty pie.
My father loves good ale,
And so do I.

Little Bob Robin,
Where do you live?
Up in yonder wood, sir,
On a hazel twig.

67

Who comes here?
A grenadier.
What do you want?
A pot of beer.
Where's your money?
I forgot it.
Get you gone,
You silly blockhead.

Oh where, oh where has my little dog gone?
Oh where, oh where can he be?
With his ears cut short and his tail cut long,
Oh where, oh where is he?

Hey ding-a-ding,
What shall I sing?
How many holes
In a skimmer?
Four-and-twenty,
My plate's empty!
Pray, Mama, give us our
Dinner.

Warm hands, warm,
The men have gone to plow.
If you want to warm your hands,
Warm your hands now.

Brush hair, brush,
The men have gone to plow.
If you want to brush your hair,
Brush your hair now.

Wash hands, wash,
The men have gone to plow.
If you want to wash your hands,
Wash your hands now.

I had a little moppet,
I kept it in my pocket
And fed it on corn and hay;
There came a proud beggar
And said he would wed her,
And stole my little moppet away.

Sally, Sally Waters
Sprinkle in the pan,
Rise, Sally, rise, Sally,
Choose a young man.
Bow to the East,
Bow to the West,
Bow to the young man
That you love best.

Now you are married
You must be good,
And help your wife
To chop the wood.
Chop it thin
And bring it in
And kiss her over
And over again.

75

The girl in the lane,
That couldn't speak plain,
Cried, Gobble, gobble, gobble.
The man on the hill,
That couldn't stand still,
Went hobble, hobble, hobble.

77

On Saturday night shall be my care
To powder my locks and curl my hair;
On Sunday morning my love will come in,
When he will marry me with a gold ring.

Cold and raw the north winds blow,
Bleak in the morning early;
All the hills are covered with snow;
And winter's now come fairly.

80

Bow, wow, wow,
Whose dog art thou?
Little Tom Tinker's dog,
Bow, wow, wow.

Go to bed late,
Stay very small;
Go to bed early,
Grow very tall.

Hark, hark,
The dogs do bark,
The beggars are coming to town;
Some in rags,
And some in jags,
And one in a velvet gown.

Christmas is coming,
The geese are getting fat,
Please put a penny
In the old man's hat.
If you haven't got a penny,
A ha'penny will do;
If you haven't got a ha'penny,
God bless you!

Jeremiah, blow the fire,
Puff, puff, puff!
First you blow it gently,
Then you blow it rough.

Up street and down street,
Each window's made of glass;
If you go to Tommy Tickler's house
You'll find a pretty lass.

Hug her and kiss her,
And take her on your knee,
And whisper very close,
Darling girl, do you love me?

Star light,
Star bright,
The first star
I see tonight,
I wish I may,
I wish I might,
Have the wish
I wish tonight.

A-hunting we will go,
A-hunting we will go,
We'll catch a fox
And put him in a box
And then we'll let him go.

I see the moon,
The moon sees me.
God bless the moon,
And God bless me.